OTHER BOOKS BY JOHN D. FREEMAN

Rockport: A Childhood by the Sea

Freedom, Tribalism, and Creativity: A Challenge to Our Syrian Friends

Jungle Episodes: A Missionary Doctor in Thailand

THE POLITICALLY INCORRECT GUIDE TO HEALTH REFORM

BY JOHN D. FREEMAN M.D.

THE POLITICALLY INCORRECT GUIDE TO HEALTH REFORM
By: John D. Freeman, M.D.

ISBN-13: 978-1495453922
ISBN-10: 1495453928

Cover and Layout Design: Ryan Oetting
Cover Image: Krista Revelle

Printed in the United States of America

"Much of the social history of the Western world, over the past 3 decades,

has been a history of replacing what worked with what sounds good."

-Thomas Sowell

CONTENTS

A BRIEF BIO
OF JOHN FREEMAN

John Freeman grew up in Rockport, Texas and received his college education in Wayland University and the University of Texas. After two years in the military his medical education was obtained in the University of South Dakota Medical School and the Univeristy of Tennessee in Memphis. Internship was in Methodist Hospital, Memphis followed by a year of surgery in Baylor Hospital, Dallas.

Overseas experience includes ten years of rural health in Thailand, two years in Saudi Arabia and a brief time with International Medical Corps in Peshawar, Pakistan. For twenty-five years John practiced emergency medicine mostly in West Tennessee. He is now retired and living in Bells, Tennessee where, with his wife Nancy, he is involved in saving rural southern history. See greenfrogtn.org.

INTRODUCTION
-CHAPTER 1-

The Washington politicians and lawyers have been trying to fix the health care system. From what I read I am not sure they know what it is that needs fixing. After forty years of working in the health field I thought I would broaden their perspective about health problems in this country. This then is a view from the bottom of the pile, so to speak, for I am a primary care physician. This means that I see the patient when he first enters the health system. My experience includes about ten years in rural Thailand where about 80% of the health problems could be solved by a nurse with immunizations, sanitation, worm pills and malaria medication. Here I have worked in rural areas (mostly West Tennessee) in family practice and emergency departments where I have observed that about 80% of disease can be cured or prevented only by determined discipline; where that commodity is lacking, then the cure is by expensive high tech medicine.

One of the Old Testament prophets spoke of being in the "Valley of Decision" (Joel 3:14) and it seems that today we are in a Valley of Decision in regards to our medical problems. The vast majority of our afflictions are no longer those over which we have no control, but are diseases of indulgence. Will the politicians continue to promote a heath welfare program that promotes self-induced poor health? As individuals we must awake to the realization that the path to good health lies in the Decision to Discipline.

In the following pages are several references to poverty, struggle and suffering. Being a doctor some may think that I know nothing of those things. I probably haven't suffered near as much as I deserve but still vivid in my memory is suffering as a stuttering child. Provoking laughter in my listeners every time my mouth was opened was enough to acquaint me with suffering disabilities. Of course, in those days there was no reward to the parents for that sort of disability, so I went to bed every night praying for deliverance which did eventually come.

The poverty I was born into was not smoothed over by a government welfare check. The earliest recollection of being poor was a conversation I overheard between my mother and two older sisters. They had been invited to a picnic and were discussing whether it would be appropriate for them to take two leftover baked sweet potatoes as their contribution. That was the only food in the house and there was no money. I worked in high school to help support the family then worked my way through college. I continued to work my way through medical school as my father was not working in those days. Being endowed with rather meager intellectual faculties, I particularly remember the struggle through medical school. It was a fight to stay awake as long as possible to study; then when sleep finally did come it was punctuated with nightmares of the anatomy cadaver or some other difficult subject. With dogged determination, one foot in front of the other, the end finally came with success.

Those of you who have health problems, read this and take heart, for many of us have suffered and struggled to overcome difficulties. Remember it can be done again and again by anyone who so chooses. So grit your teeth and read on. You may find that some of your problems can be fixed before the politicians get to them.

WHY THE WORLD WOBBLES (PROBLEMS OF OBESITY)
-CHAPTER 2-

Sometime in the late 70's, while working in an emergency room in North Carolina, I was struck by the dramatic change in the physique of patients from those to which I had grown accustomed in the jungles of Thailand. The nurse informed me that a late-night patient was ready to be seen. Down the hall I caught a glimpse of the massive form of a woman who having been seated upon the examining bed assumed the form of a pyramid as the fat settled into its resting configuration.

There weren't any fat people in rural Thailand in those days. Well, there was one exception in the small town of Bangkla where we worked for a while. One of the market ladies was so obese that she had to be hauled to the market each day in a pushcart. She sold sweets and it appeared that she cleaned up all the leftovers at the end of the day. That was the exception, but here in the States the exception is getting to be a thin person. The past few weeks I have been reading some grim statistics in the papers. One-third of all children are now overweight and one-half of all adults are obese. In the past seven years the people in the age group around thirty have gained an average of ten pounds each! The trend is still in the upward direction so the worst is yet to come. With our tremendous weight gain in this country the world will begin to wobble.

These fat people are sitting on our health care system and beginning to squeeze the life out of it. Just think what the situation will be in ten or twenty years from now. Don't get complacent. We live in a democracy where the majority rules, and guess who that will be. Why is obesity squeezing the life out of the health care system you ask? Just look at the diseases that obesity begets; heart disease, hypertension, diabetes, arthritis and cancer. Note that these are the high cost items in health care eating up tons of your tax dollars when the patient is in the health welfare system. Of course there are many other diseases to which obesity contributes.

Perhaps disabilities should be mentioned here. Already there are thousands in the U.S that are disabled solely due to their obesity. Now think what will happen in a few years when the obese are in a distinct majority in the country. Obesity will be voted in as a legitimate form of disability creating a stampede on the supermarkets as hundreds and thousands will be increasing their weight in order to qualify for disability and free food stamps. Hospital and nursing home workers wrestling with obese patients are frequently disabled from back injuries incurred while moving or lifting these patients.

If we are going to make an attempt to overcome this problem of obesity, the first thing that needs to be done is to find out what causes it. The other day I was talking to an obese patient about the need to lose some of her cargo and she responded by saying, "Doctor you wouldn't believe what I eat." I thought to myself, "Yes I would." Then she went on to say, "I don't eat anything!" I had heard that statement many times before I finally figured out that they were saying, "I don't eat any thing compared to what I would really like to eat."

The mysterious etiology of this malady of which we are speaking is indeed a problem for those so affected. The other day I was trying to impress upon a seriously affected patient who had diabetes as well as hypertension (scars on the abdomen indicated previous gallbladder surgery and hysterectomy) the need to shed pounds as the path to better health. "But doctor," she replied, "don't you think heredity has a lot to do with it?" She was very serious and seemed to be genuinely searching for the answer to the mystery. Other patients have asked the same question only with hormones in place of heredity. Not being very busy at the time I carefully explained to her that everyone since Adam has been afflicted with heredity as well as hormones. Then I asked her if she had seen the television program about the refugees from the current African crisis. "Why are all those people very thin?' I asked. Quick as a wink her chubby daughter replied, "Because they don't have enough to eat."

The rapid answer from the daughter gave me cause to think that I had gained ground on that great mystery and within me there was a slight glow of satisfaction in my battle to enlighten the world. Then I looked again at the overweight patient and her look made me realize that she was still under the spell of the megamystery of medical maladies. I looked at the daughter and contrary to my usual spirit of optimism realized that she too would in a few years lose her youthful wisdom and become engulfed in that awesome mysterious mist.

Back to the daughter's answer. Obesity is a very simple matter. If one doesn't eat too much then one doesn't get overweight. Put in another set of simple terms, If you weigh too much then you eat too much regardless of how much you eat and yes regardless of heredity and hormones.

Appetite is usually a dominant factor in obesity and to control that we must use our discipline. If you refuse to use your discipline then stop begging others to pay your monstrous medical bills. Remember this is something you brought on yourself. Obesity is the result of deliberate coordinated usually complex efforts on the part of those afflicted.

A SLOW BURN AND
A SACK FULL OF MEDICINE

-CHAPTER 3-

One morning when I had left most of my bedside manners at home I was called to see a woman in her early forties who wanted her medicines refilled. A quick glance over the chart revealed that she was an insulin dependent diabetic who the previous year had heart bypass surgery. She had a brown paper bag full of medicine bottles sitting beside her. With a glance at her face and a listen to her voice I asked her how much she smoked. "I'm cutting down." she replied which is the smokers equivalent to the obese person's "I don't eat anything."

I picked up the bag and started going through the

medicines. There were two types of medicine for emphysema. It was explained that if she didn't smoke she would not need those. Next were two kinds of expensive blood pressure medicines. Again it was explained to her that if she stopped smoking she might be able to cut out some of the antihypertensives. A bottle of nerve pills was next. Smoking damages and irritates the nervous system so that medicine could be eliminated if she stopped lighting up. By that time I noted that she was beginning to get color into that smoker's pallid complexion but as I said my bedside manners were left at home that day so I went to the next bottle which was an anti-ulcer medication. Smoking irritates the stomach and promotes ulcers and prevents healing so that bit of information was explained to the now agitated patient.

It was in Thailand that I cut my teeth in the practice of medicine. I hadn't been there long before I realized the value of preventive medicine and how cheap preventive medicine was compared to curative medicine. When I explained to the rural Thai patients how to prevent malaria or intestinal worms or whatever they seemed genuinely appreciative. Somehow I haven't gotten the knack of being appreciated as I try to practice preventive medicine on these American self-induced diseases.

The diabetic smoker really blew a fuse when I suggested to her that the expensive heart surgery was largely the result of her smoking habit. It was her time to talk so I listened as she aimed a few choice phrases at me. Realizing I had said too much I remained quiet until her raspy voice was silent then she collected herself and in a slow burn grabbed her sack full of medicines and marched out the door vowing to go to another medical facility where she would be treated more kindly.

I have found the sack full of medicine to be an almost constant companion of the smoker or the obese patient. When I see ten or twelve bottles of medicine lined up beside a chart I expect the patient to be a smoker and that is generally true. However when I see on the chart that the patient is up in the eighties and nineties and there are no medicine bottles then I know that the patient is non-obese and a nonsmoker. My father was a good example of that. He remained thin all his life, exercised and didn't smoke. He outlived all the other smoking men in our neighborhood by at least twenty years and at last died after a short illness at age ninety-four.

When I do something naughty I usually get into

trouble, and sure enough about two weeks later there was a letter in my box from the hospital administrator scolding me for having bad bedside manners. Included was the letter from the diabetic smoker demanding that the hospital not pay me for that visit and furthermore demanding that her "insurance" not be billed for that visit. Of course that "insurance" was government welfare and so was coming out of my pocket as well as yours if you are a working taxpayer. I needed my job so I confessed to the administrator that I had been unkind to a diabetic smoker with multiple self-induced diseases who was costing the taxpayer bundles of money for her foolishness. To be honest though, if it weren't for smokers and fat people I would be out of a job or would have a very skimpy income.

Productive cough and sinus problems summed up the nurse's notes on the chart. After listening to the young lady's problems I asked her how much she smoked. "How did you know I smoked?' she exclaimed. "I caught a glimpse of you as you came in the ER." I replied. "How can you tell just by looking?" she went on. I explained to her that after several years of smoking the skin assumes a pasty gray color which I call a corpse-like-countenance. She was invited to notice the skin on a corpse at the next funeral and then go look in the mirror. Her eyes widened and wrinkles of concern formed on her forehead; then she declared that she was certainly quitting smoking. Hopefully I had redeemed myself in that encounter but the administrative merit badge never showed up. A few months later at another place I met the lady and she asked me how she looked after stopping that habit.

Smoking is not just physically debilitating, but it is also a road to the poorhouse. It is usually the poor who smoke to begin with as the habit consumes a higher percentage of their income. The smoker is usually a cola addict; put those two together and the yearly cost is rather large. The smoker is less healthy, weaker and therefore is of less value to the employer or to himself if he is self-employed. The end result is that his habit keeps him poor. Of the twenty-five percent of the population that smoke look where they are in the economic spectrum. Naturally they sink to the bottom. The obese have a similar sinking problem. Almost every health welfare patient I see is a smoker or if one is a child, the parents smoke.

Dear Abby recently gave some statistics that illustrate the enormity of the problem of smoking. In her column she stated that lung cancer is the leading cause of death in both women and men resulting in 153,000 deaths per year. Other smoking related diseases such as heart and lung take away another 419,000 people a year. Adverse effects of smoking costs the country over $100 billion per year in medical costs and economic loss.

One could go on all day about smoking related problems but the point to be made here is that we are paying fantastic sums of money (tax money) to cure the effects of smoking. The interesting matter here is that the smoker has no responsibility to pay for his self-induced illnesses while he is on government health welfare. He can keep on picking the pockets of the working taxpayer as long as he likes with no restrictions. I have a hard time seeing the justice in such wealth redistribution.

COKES, CONSTIPATION AND COLON CANCER
-CHAPTER 4-

In thirty years of medical practice the most frightening experience was the time I re-entered practice here in the States after seven years in a mission hospital in the jungles of Thailand. For seven years I hadn't seen a heart attack, diabetes, colon cancer, hypertension, obesity, gallbladder disease, or diverticulitis. Then suddenly I was surrounded daily by people dropping with heart attacks, diabetic comas, strokes, gallbladder attacks, diverticulitis and hypertensive crisis, severe emphysema etc. I could heal all the diseases I had seen in rural Thailand with a knife or a pill, but these diseases that surrounded me here in the States were chronic progressive problems that eventually devoured a person's health. What was the difference in my patients in Thailand and these here in the States? That question plagued me.

In preparing to take the Family Practice Board Exam I attended a refresher seminar at the University of Tennessee in Memphis that Fall of 1977. During one of the luncheon meetings a videotape program of Dr. Dennis Burkett was presented. I was completely fascinated by his story of working in East Africa for many years then returning to practice in England. He had experienced the same shock I was going through, but being a surgeon, it was surgical diseases that concerned him. The thing that impressed him the most was the epidemic of colon cancer in England and the fact that he had seen none in Africa. His inquiries led him to postulate that a refined diet (low fiber) was an important contribution to the discrepancy in the disease patterns. He conducted some interesting studies as he traveled the world studying the diets and measuring the daily stool volume and gastrointestinal transit times of primitive rural people compared to citified peoples on refined diets.

Dr. Burkett's studies led him to the conclusion that the type of food we eat has much to do with the diseases we acquire. Since the diseases absent in my Thai patients were similar to those absent in his African patients and since both groups of people were eating unrefined foods for the most part I agreed with him and began to modify my eating habits accordingly. Trying to be a good missionary I preach this to my patients as well.

One doesn't have to be a doctor to realize that what we eat has a tremendous influence on our health. One day when my Dad was nearing ninety he and Nancy, my wife, were engaged in a conversation about various matters. He leaned over in all seriousness and asked her if she knew what the greatest problem in the country was. Expecting a profound commentary on a social or political matter Nancy was rather taken aback when he answered simply "Its constipation." We laughed about that a lot but if you don't believe there is truth in that statement just find out how many billions are spent to correct that malady in this country alone, then find out how many billions are spent of your tax dollars just to correct the matter in government sponsored nursing home patients.

Dr. Burkett's stool studies exposed the cause of a lot of our problems but the veil of resistance to the truth still prevails. If you don't believe it go to the grocery store and see how much white fiberless bread there is compared to the whole wheat bread. Then go to the nursing homes and hospitals and watch them feed white bread and macaroni with cheese then give them all a deconstipator at bedtime. But even those bedtime pills don't always do the job so we in the emergency department are frequented with requests for "digital extraction procedures." No, that's not anything kin to a CAT scan; it is just the old fashioned finger way to remove a hard fecal plug to regain regularity. I even saw one patient so plugged his whole colon had to be removed.

Well, enough about the sluggish bowel syndrome or I will be accused of being a fixated old man. This condition is expensive enough in itself and also contributes to colon cancer, hiatal hernia, diverticulitis and hemorrhoids. It is an entirely-self induced and preventable condition if one will simply eat the proper foods and they are usually the most economical foods as well.

Before leaving this subject I will pass on Dr. Burkett's formula for a happy stooler. The stool should be bulky and float in the water (floaters). Then the transit time should be 24 hours or less. Oh one more thing, they should pass with ease. When you have achieved this there will be no need to tell others for they will know by your countenance.

In case you haven't caught on this chapter is about eating disorders and I don't mean bulemia and that sort of thing, I mean simply eating the wrong things that make us sick. The other day a young patient came in escorted by his mother. He was complaining about feeling bad with palpitations and dizziness. I asked him what he thought caused the problem but he didn't know. Next I asked him what he had been doing the night before but the answer was nothing particular. Then my onboard breathalyzer prompted me to ask how much he had drunk the night before, a six pack or half case? His response was closer to a half case. Smoking was the next question and the answer to this was about two packs per day. The next query was concerning cokes of which about eight to ten were consumed daily. After examining the patient and not finding any abnormality I turned to the anxious mother and asked her if it didn't seem that he was suffering from an overdose of drugs; caffeine, alcohol, and tobacco. I could tell by the mother's pasty gray complexion that she was a tobacco addict as well, so the young man came by his habits honestly.

There seems to be an alarming increase in people who

never drink water but consume only sugared drinks. This frequent overdosing on pure sugar causes a rapid rise in blood sugar resulting in spikes of insulin release which then results in a reactive sugar decline in the blood. Just how much damage this sugar overloading causes ultimately, I don't know, but it is not unusual to have patients complaining of dizziness and no cause is determined except heavy sugared drink consumption. This is just another example of unwise eating habits and a very costly habit as well.

A while back there was another patient with a similar story. He was about twenty-five and had been given a prescription for hypertension. He returned with blood pressure sky high so I asked about the antihypertensive medicine I had ordered. He replied that he didn't get it as he wanted to save money. Both he and his wife smoked, they never drank water, only cokes and moreover they ate at fast-food places all the time so one can imagine the cost. He was too "frugal" to pay for a five dollar prescription for a life saving medicine. Imagine what the fast-food, hi-fat, and hi-salt diet was doing to his hypertension.

Enough said about the diet disorders of the American people. The point I am trying to make here is that the diseases caused by our poor nutrition are costing billions and are self-induced and entirely preventable. Is it right or reasonable for the person who steadfastly refuses to maintain a disciplined diet to demand his health care at the expense of those who live sensibly?

ILLEGITIMACY AIDS AND INNOCENCE

-CHAPTER 5-

After completing the examination of the fourteen year old school girl I informed her and her mother that I doubted that the kick in the belly had injured the first trimester pregnancy. Then I asked her why her boyfriend had kicked her. She explained that he became upset when told that the pregnancy was not the result of his endeavors. This was a rather dramatic reminder of what I had read in the papers about the cult of certain American males who prove their manhood by getting as many girls pregnant as possible. I suppose the person becomes a type of hero when a certain number of notches are on his counter.

For my purpose here I am defining illegitimacy as one of the diseases of sexual promiscuity. Whether you agree with me or not is irrelevant for the point here is that illegitimacy is a major cause of poverty, of poor education and crime in the country today. The psychological diseases of a child brought into the world into such circumstances are enormous and very costly to our health system. The physical and psychological problems of the unwed mother are staggering as well.

If you will examine the influence of the entertainment and news industry you will get an idea where much of the responsibility for this mushrooming problem lies. Higher education has had its influence as well. It is interesting that some cultures don't have this problem. Recently I was talking to a young Thai man in Chiang Mai and our conversation got around to AIDS in his village. He said that there was none in his village. I asked for an explanation when there was so much in the large cities in Thailand. He replied simply, "In our village we treat all the girls as sisters." Then later I was telling a Karen (one of the Hill tribe people in Thailand) about the millions of people in our country who don't know who their father is. He questioned me carefully about my statement then said emphatically, "Every Karen knows who their father is!"

Then with wonderment in his voice asked, "What kind of place would it be not to know who your father is?"

Center stage today of the diseases caused by sexual promiscuity is AIDS that dreaded enigma of the those who envisioned free sex as the centerpiece of their hedonistic religion. The fear of HIV virus has caused untold millions in increased health costs as we have had to take severe precautions to protect ourselves and our patients from that deadly disease. The increased costs of blood and blood products testing has added billions of dollars in just that area. Don't forget we still have to test for several of the older sexually transmitted diseases such as syphilis and the various types of hepatitis. The costs of the long term treatment of AIDS patients and their disability is astronomical and getting greater by the day.

There are a host of other sexually transmitted diseases such as herpes, gonorrhea, clymadia and others. In the past few years it has been shown that the sexually transmitted human papilloma virus is responsible for the greater part of cervical cancer in women. Testing for cervical cancer in women (Pap Test) would probably be unnecessary if it weren't for sexually transmitted diseases thus saving hundreds of millions in health costs. Treatment costs for the sexually transmitted diseases are among one of the major items in the federal health budget.

One could go on all day haranguing about the horrors of hedonism, but again the point to be made here is that sexually promiscuous diseases are basically self-induced except for those innocently infected by a promiscuous partner or a blood transfusion. In a government health care system those who indulge in hedonistic pleasures want the morally disciplined to pick up the tab for their joy ride.

THEY OUGHT TO FILL THAT HOLE IN THE ROAD
-CHAPTER 6-

About the time on a Saturday night when the spirits were flowing freely and there had been sufficient time for them to exert their influence, a young lady was brought into the emergency room. As our small E. R. was filled with other matters of a serious nature that night I did a quick evaluation of the patient. Everything checked out all right except three deep and long lacerations to the scalp caused by the head hitting the windshield. As I examined her she kept saying, "They ought to fill that hole in the road."

About two hours later, after the other patients had been cared for and the head wounds sewed up to the tune of repeated lines of "They ought to fill that hole in the road." we finally had the emergency cleaned out. While finishing up some paper work the nurse asked me if I knew what that hole in the road was. "Well, I figured it must have been a ditch. What was it?" I replied. The nurse then explained that the patient had made a wrong turn at the railroad tracks, went up on a loading ramp, then ran off the end of it and hit a pile of cross ties. I chuckled a bit and admitted that a pothole of that nature did need fixing.

A few days later the Emergency Medical Service brought in a young man and his older uncle. An automobile accident they said as they unloaded the two. I went over the pair and found not too much wrong other than some superficial lacerations and bruises. Having completed the exam I inquired of the EMS personnel as to the circumstances of the accident. As near as they could figure out the two had been out in the forest cutting wood and had the pickup filled and ready to go home. The uncle who had been sipping from a bottle off and on all day decided that a designated driver was needed so appointed his nephew. They had just started across a field when the driver had an epileptic fit and in such a state he stiffened up jamming his foot on the accelerator.

The truck raced down a hill cutting a path through a groove of saplings for a quarter of a mile then came face to face with a granddaddy oak tree. When the EMS arrived, wood was scattered around and both nephew and uncle had sobered substantially. Fortunately the saplings slowed their journey to the extent that no great injury occurred to either. Well, so much for the designated driver.

Alcohol occasionally has a bit of humor associated with it but far more often the Devil is in the driver's seat and a heap of misery is left along the road he drives.

The other day a young lady came in with what turned out to be a minor condition but in the course of getting her history I found an interesting story. She was a recovering alcoholic and proud of eight years of sobriety. Her husband, also an alcoholic, was walking the straight and narrow with her. A happy and peaceful disposition in a person with such a history naturally incurred my curiosity so I pried into her past. Both parents had been afflicted as well and were killed by a drunk driver when the young lady was at a tender young age. Such tragedy in her life only mystified me more as to her smiling countenance. "I have to be well by Thursday." she said at the end of the conversation. "Why is that ?' I wanted to know. "Because I have to cook for the AA group. My husband and I help with our local AA and it is our time to prepare a meal for about fifty people."

When I was growing up alcohol was the major addictive substance but such is not the case today. There is a host of addictive substances now including legal prescription drugs and illegal street drugs. A major cause of all this addiction is in the disruption of families with the resulting psychological instability. As a child I also remember that divorce was something to be ashamed of, and when mentioned the word was whispered. It is accepted that one of the greatest risk factors for addiction is family discord/disruption but the liberal news and entertainment media as well as much of the educational system still promotes the type of behavior that leads to such suffering. It also does all it can to berate the forces that promote morality.

Jim is a patient that I have become very well acquainted with over the past ten years of working in West Tennessee emergency departments. When I first met Jim he had just shot himself in the foot, accidentally as he said but, according to my sources it was intentional as a way to get prescription drugs. Being of a rather suspicious nature about situations like that I was reluctant to give narcotics. Needless to say he went away rather disgruntled mumbling, "You will hear from my lawyer"

The next time I met Jim it was in another city where he turned up in the emergency complaining of pain in his foot. Infection had set in where he had shot himself. He was admitted to the hospital for treatment of the infection. In the end the foot had to be amputated. Jim left the hospital in "hog heaven" as we say down South, for he now would be eligible for a monthly disability check as well as government health welfare. Now he could buy the drugs off the street as well as badger the emergency departments and doctors offices for prescription drugs.

Sure enough Jim kept coming to the emergency and I kept seeing him but not giving him any drugs. He kept coming though because other doctors would give him the drugs he wanted just to get him out of their hair or because they felt sorry for him. He mentioned one doctor's office where he could go anytime he wanted and get his favorite, Percodan. With a Percodan, a Valium, and a Coke he could lift his feet off the ground and soar with the eagles. A large smile would come across his face as he relived in his mind that pure pleasure of a drug high. By this time we had become "good friends" so he would give me a lot of true information mixed in with his drug seeking garbage.

Jim came in once with skin infections all over his arms and legs the result of "skin popping." That is when the addict injects the narcotic just under the skin when he has used up all his veins. The last time I saw Jim he informed me that he had stopped using drugs and was working at a regular job. "And how did that come about?" I wanted to know. "I just decided that I had had enough" he replied.

There are a lot of Jims out there in the drug world, many that are worse than he and scads more that are not so bad but torment the daylights out of doctors in their offices and in emergency rooms as they seek their highs. I wouldn't dare to estimate the money that is wasted on drug seeking behavior but needless to say it is a sizable sum when we add up the total from all the hospitals and clinics across the country. Guess who pays for all this?

Drug and alcohol abuse has other costs as well. It is the greatest cause of industrial accidents. Alcohol figures in close to half of all traffic fatalities in the country. It is a factor in most of the domestic violence. Our youths are at greatest risk of death from traffic accidents and most of those are influenced by drugs or alcohol. Recently there appeared in the medical literature reports of how wine will decrease heart attacks in men. That may be so but a few extra years in some men seems an awful lopsided comparison to all the devastation alcohol causes. Better to not eat so much fat than to have to drink Drano to clean out the plumbing.

How did Jim quit drugs? He decided. The important thing to remember about alcohol and drug abuse is that it is a disease of decision just like all the other self-induced diseases. There has been a lot made of alcohol genes and the part heredity plays. Just yesterday I heard on television about a new fat gene. Sure, we will find a gene for every one of our self-induced diseases sooner or later. We cannot do anything about the genes but spend money to find them but we can all make decisions. We can choose not to use drugs, and if we get addicted to a substance, we can choose to stop or get help from one of those wonderful organizations like the Alcoholics Anonymous. There is plenty of help out there if a person will but admit that he needs it and chooses to go after it.

Speaking about the AA got me to thinking about that sweet little lady who was a recovering alcoholic. I think that the key to her happiness was that she and her husband had become involved in helping others. It occurred to me that helping others was what Jesus was trying to teach us to do more than anything else. He said something of the order that if we seek life we will lose it and if we lose it for His sake we will find it. Isn't that what the happy lady had discovered? Finding a cure for my own problem by helping someone else? Go ahead and give it a try. That may be the best way yet to fill up the potholes in our roads.

THE CORPULENT CARDIAC

-CHAPTER 7-

The abnormal EKG tracings on the monitor were occupying my attention as the thrombolytic drugs dissolved the blood clots in the heart and caused what is known as reperfusion beats. The middle aged man had arrived in the emergency room within a couple hours of the heart attack which occurred while he was walking his dog. It had been touch and go for a while as his blood pressure dropped then responded to medications only to develop a rapid heart rate. Each complication responded to the drugs administered and he responded with, "Am I going to die?" The attentive and kind nurse reassured him each time that everything would be all right.

As the clots continued to dissolve another group of irregular beats occurred on the monitor. That cluster of irregular beats in rapid succession caused the heart to quiver a bit, prompting the man to anxiously ask again, "Am I going to die?' It was then that I became more aware of the corpulent cardiac patient's concerns than I had been of what was going on in his cardiovascular system. The question came across my mind as to why he was so concerned with dying now when for years he had no such thoughts as indicated by the state of his body. I further surmised that he was probably more concerned with the dog's need to exercise than of his own need for the exercise.

Having been reassured again by the nurse a calm settled over the scene as the heart tracing assumed a normal pattern. Another look at the sad shape of our patient caused me to began to paint a picture of his daily activities. On the floor with a couple of other belongings was a cane left there by the ambulance crew. That told me that he was on welfare disability which meant that he sat around all day. Walking the dog broke the boredom a bit. He may even have a riding lawn mower which he would use once a week. There would be at least one trip to the store a day to get the "sedentary sitter's" essential supplies, sodas and cigarettes. Of course when he went to the store he would park as close to the entrance as possible to prevent any unnecessary steps. Most of the day would be occupied watching television, with a channel changer in his hand to prevent inconvenient ups and downs.

One of the regular chores included trips to the doctor's office or to the emergency room to get his pain and sleep medications refilled. Sleep doesn't come easy with all the sitting and slumbering during the day. The sedentary's life crawls along at a slow pace only to be interrupted now and then by something exciting. Our Corpulent Cardiac will enjoy his present episode as well as the following activities which will include a cardiac catheterization followed more than likely by a heart bypass operation. He will really be disabled then and that will bring a great deal of satisfaction.

The other day I was reading an article in the Family Practice Journal that mentioned exercise as the "medicine" that, if taken regularly, was the single most effective means of preventing cardiovascular disease. That includes heart disease, hypertension and stroke. The shame about this is that the "medicine" is so seldom used even though it is entirely free. But like the old saying, "That which is free is not appreciated."

Inactivity is worshipped today as though it were a religion by a large segment of the population. According to some studies more than 50% of the population are adherents to this sedentary worship. The favorite altar is the television. In the late fifties I taught school a year and at that time children were already seated in front of the altar of inactivity three to four and more hours a day. Labor saving devices are lusted after and incorporated into this worship program with gusto.

Not only are the cardiovascular diseases prevented and improved by exercise but other conditions are helped as well. It has long been known that mental depression is greatly alleviated by regular vigorous exercise. Just the other day I was reading that exercise in young girls is associated with less breast cancer when they grow to adulthood. I wouldn't be surprised if we find that almost all cancer is influenced by exercise for in the rural areas of Thailand I found cancer to be practically nonexistent in that population which gets a healthy amount of physical exercise. Naturally the musculoskeletal system is greatly affected by exercise. Osteoporosis is much decreased by activity. In ten years in Thailand never did I see a broken hip in a person even though many live to be elderly.

It is not a secret that regular activity is associated with longevity. A few years ago I was examining an elderly man of about ninety years who had a febrile illness of some kind. I asked the son about his past illnesses. "Nothing to speak of. He has never been to a doctor." he answered. "Dad put in a crop with a mule up until a couple of years ago. He quit then only because the mule died." Even Alzheimer's Disease is less severe in those who are more active.

The thing that amazes me is how creative the lazy person can be in finding ways of avoiding exertional activity. The "do what feels good" permissive culture of today doesn't help things any along this line either. Just think what it is going to cost the health system to keep the Corpulent Cardiac going just a little longer. All those expenses so unnecessary if he had just a little discipline. He doesn't want to die neither does he want to discipline so he calls, "Do all you can Doc!" knowing it is not a dime of his money going down the drain. We did all we could and the politician will do all he can to help, but one question remains. Is it right for those who sink into the sedentary to seek the sympathy of those who work at a disciplined life?

SLIPPERY STEPS

-CHAPTER 8-

There I stood behind the patient looking at the four stab wounds in his chest. Being of a curious nature and liking to have a bit of entertainment along with my work I inquired of the patient as to the circumstances of his predicament. He started out the explanation in what sounded to me a logical answer then abruptly stopped and said, "Doc, it was like this, I was about to go downstairs with a butcher knife in my hand when suddenly I slipped. When I got up at the bottom of the stairs there were these four stab wounds in my back."

While patching up those wounds I began reading between the lines to reconstruct the "circumstances." I'll let you draw your own conclusions, but it seems that his wounds resulted from rather careless and foolish pursuits. Having been around in medicine a while it has occurred to me that a vast amount of our problems result from carelessness and foolishness moreover it seems that many people seem to enjoy such activity. One of my first live assignments in my Memphis medical school was to get a medical history from an old "Riverboat Gambler" as he called himself. I was stumped when he admitted to having had lead poisoning three times. Being young and naive I asked for an explanation. "Well the first time it was a .44, the next time it was a .38 and then I took a little .22." I caught on to his "lead poisoning." Next I asked him why he was stopping all those bullets. He was more honest than the above patient as he was further removed from the "circumstances" so he answered, "The same old story, wine, women and song."

One morning I was carefully and tediously sewing up some severe face lacerations on an older patient who had been driving without a seatbelt when his car rear-ended another at a stop light. I asked him why he didn't wear his seatbelt when that was the law and it would have saved him a lot of trouble. He replied, "I'm too old to change."

Whereupon I countered, "If you are not too old to change your face then why should you be too old to change your mind?" He made an unhappy sounding grunt so I decided not to go on in that vein. Such unnecessary injuries go on by the thousands all over the country every day.

An experience from my first year in practice still is as vivid as it is painful. Dr. Jim DeGeest took me out in the country from our little Miller, SD clinic to investigate a fatal accident. At the scene a young lifeless mother lay with hardly a scratch on her. The car had flipped throwing her out then rolling over on her. The car was hardly damaged. A simple seat belt would have prevented that calamity but that was in the days when belts were just coming into use.

As soon as I walked into the room the glowering icy stare of the older woman caught my attention. Standing next to her was a younger pregnant woman. Then I focused my attention on the young man on the examining table. A four-wheeler accident. "Nothing wrong," I explained to the women, "just a broken femur and a fractured forearm." Then I began to feel vibrations emanating from the older woman as a tear trickled down the cheek of the pregnant one. I tried vainly to say something to defuse the situation but disaster was in the air. The new baby was due any day and here the husband, the son of the glowering one, would be unable to be of any use. Again stupidity had soured the situation.

One could go on all day about all the needless injuries and illnesses that we bring on ourselves that could have been prevented by a little common sense. This multibillion dollar drain on the health care system must be stretched out over everyone that gets into the system whether we like it or not. In a government health welfare system we end up subsidizing the stupidity of carelessness.

There are other forms of injuries and illnesses that we bring on ourselves that are of a more subtle nature. Living alone is one of the disease producing situations that would fit into this category. There was one patient that I had who had to make a clinic visit at least once a week for her hypochondriacal complaints. Needless to say she lived alone and didn't get much tender loving care. I haven't seen any study about the costs in medical care of living alone but it must be an enormous sum as well as all the other household expenses.

In Thailand one of the American diseases that I

never had the occasion to think about (with one exception) is Alzheimer's Disease. It is said that this disease is rare as hen's teeth in China as well. Both of these societies have the extended family basically intact. I visited one of our leprosy patients once in Bangkok and found a child in the home that seemed to be younger than he would have had. I inquired if it was his child. "Oh, no." he replied, "We just took her to raise. You know, no home is complete without a child and an old person." What beautiful words!

When someone else is paying for the consequences of our foolish actions it makes it a lot easier to continue along the same concourse.

SUFFERING OF THE SOUL

-CHAPTER 9-

Dr. Sam and I were seated in the dining room having lunch together and making small talk in the process. Somehow the conversation drifted into the subject of divorce and family problems Not knowing anything about the family life of the doctors in the hospital where I had began working as an emergency physician I related to Dr. Sam the summary of a newspaper article I had recently read. It said that divorce affects children so adversely that the death of a parent was better tolerated than divorce. Dr. Sam was silent for a moment then responded with, "In that case I would be better off dead." That caught me off guard then he went on.

"My wife and I have only recently completed our divorce."

Naturally that turn of the conversation left me with an uneasy feeling, but the fact of the matter is that the news article is true. Kicking the psychological foundation from under children(of any age) starts in motion a suffering of the soul that lingers for life. In some cases it may go on into the next generations for didn't one of the prophets observe that the sins of the fathers are passed on to even the fifth generation. That is not a curse from God but simply another manifestation of reaping what we sow.

Of course, it is not only the fathers that leave the families these days. After returning from Thailand in 1977 our pastor mentioned in a conversation that mothers leave families these days in the same numbers as fathers. Nancy and I found that hard to believe then, but as the years have passed our experience in what we have observed has led us to the same conclusion.

The other night about one in the morning I was called in to see a young weeping wife. Her eyes were bloodshot and the eyelids and surrounding face was bruised and swollen. One look at her and I knew what had happened. The drunk husband had come in from a party and for no good reason picked an argument and then began his battering session. Such abuse is not an uncommon occurence, but remember that we only see the tip of the iceburg as most women are too ashamed of what happens to let it be known. Domestic violence generates an untold amount of silent suffering.

It seems that women comprise the majority of the sufferers but there are men who suffer as well. We had just completed irrigating the stomach of a 65 year old man who had taken sixty psychothropic tablets. I had noticed the obviously depressed look of a silent sufferer. When we were finished with our little procedures I had time to go talk with the patient. After a long marriage and having raised several children the wife decided to leave. The divorce had recently been finalized. A holiday season was coming up throwing the man who was nearing retirement into a deep depression.

Domestic discord, as everyone knows, is of unbelievable proportions today. The diseases that we bring on ourselves are bad enough but those that we inflict on others for the sake of our own pleasure or our "right to be happy," as we hear so often, is the saddest of all.

Late one night I was carefully sewing up several deep

lacerations on the wrist of a young lady who had given up on keeping things together. At first I was disgruntled at what I thought was unnecessary sewing, but I began to question the pretty girl about the circumstances leading up to her great unhappiness. Our conversation, as it went on, changed into counseling with a few lessons from the Great Physician woven into the stitching. She opened up her heart which had accumulated a lot of sadness and hurt for a young lady her age. Somewhere along the way, the parents, perhaps even the grandparents had chosen passing pleasures over duty and inflicted a lingering suffering on that one that they presumed to love.

There are many visits to the emergency room resulting from domestic upheaval that are of a rather trivial nature but that eat up a serious amount of money. One of these is what I call the Sunday night syndrome. Usually it's the mother who brings the child to the emergency room after he has spent the weekend with the father and his new wife. The mother in her bitterness wants to point her finger at the father as having abused the child in some way or as being responsible for the child's cold symptoms. Rarely is there anything of serious nature wrong with the child, and if the mother were paying for the visit needless to say it would never occur. Government welfare is what pays for the visit which means you and your working friends. There are several other variations played out on this theme of demonstrating injury of some nature to accuse an enemy.

It is bad enough for these games to be played between two consenting adults, but it is even worse when children get caught in these angry retaliatory tangles. It is in such a milieu that the child's learning often takes place and this learning is more by osmosis than by, "Do what I say." The child then has built into his personality the seeds of depression, despair and physical disease. We continually hear that about one-half of all marriages end in divorce, about one-third of children are born out of wedlock and one-fourth of children live in fatherless homes. What seeds of disease we are sowing for physical and social ills!

The resulting damage to the child whether from divorce or from inter-family fighting is often permanent and impossible to calculate in its monetary cost. When the psychological and moral foundations of a person have been fragmented, then that child will be more prone to eating disorders, smoking addiction, drug and alcohol abuse, sexual promiscuity and crime. It is those conditions and the diseases that they spawn where a great expenditure of health dollars are required. And of course, eventually the child's marriage will be jeopardized. Even learning is seriously affected as the late Alan Bloom described in his insightful book "The Closing of the American Mind." The child as he matures has the right to choose his own course, but the choosing of the parents holds a powerful influence.

Chapter after chapter and book after book could be written about the disastrous effects of family discord on the physical and mental health not to mention the effect on the social and non-medical economic aspects of our society. This is another type of disease of our own choosing. As with alcoholism our own choosing often affects innocent others. Somehow in a health system paid for by the taxpayer some mechanism should be built into it that would induce a sense of responsibility in the members of the system to live according to duty and not decadence. However, in our present system and in those proposed by the government such is not the case. People are rewarded for being poor by receiving cash awards, and rewarded for sexual promiscuity by receiving cash subsidies for illegitimate children. Those sitting idle are given money to smoke with and food stamps to get fat with. Disease is rewarded with generous disability checks. Where is the incentive to be healthy and reasonable?

THE JACKPOT MENTALITY

-CHAPTER 10-

Theresa, the ER nurse, called me over to look at the TV screen that monitored the door of the Emergency department. Paul was dancing in a circle waving in the air his prescription for Percodan, a strong pain reliever, that he had just conned me out of. He had limped into the hospital that night complaining of having been kicked in the chest by a mule and having terrible pain. After the exam there was a bit of suspicion but my guard was down so contrary to my usual practice I gave him the narcotic pain reliever. Theresa knowing how I feel about drug seekers was having a good laugh at my expense. Chagrined at Paul's lying deceitful behavior I said, "He really hit the jackpot tonight!" for I had given him a pain shot as well. Within a few minutes he and his significant other would be off to another ER to play bingo again.

After Theresa had stopped making fun of me I picked up Paul's chart to add a few pertinent remarks. I noted that he had a Medicaid number but it was no use trying to tell anyone. They are not interested in that kind of information about their patients. I had talked to the hospital administrator about the problem once but he was not interested either. Never mind just let the paying patient pick up the tab. Paul would be out on the street selling the Percodan within a couple hours for a healthy profit.

A patient I knew a few years back needed an operation with a price tag of about $3,000. He was not rich but neither was he poor, for he had money to get a new car when needed and buy a new house as well as other necessities. After getting a careful medical history I estimated that about $5,000 were spent yearly on cigarettes, colas, beer and other entertainment. He didn't want to spend money on an essential item like health so off he went to sign up for Medicaid which was approved. Another Jackpot!

There are plenty of other Jackpot winners who daily take

home their bonanzas. Disability is one of the popular games of bingo today. When I was young it was the old and feeble who used canes; now it is the badge of the disabled or those playing the game and waiting to yell Jackpot! I could almost count on one hand all the truly disabled I have seen.

A friend told about his experience in the supermarket the other day. He was in line at the checkout counter behind an obese family with a loaded cart. When the checker informed the customer that food stamps would not pay for dog food the mother instructed one of the children to return the sack of dog food and get that five pound package of ground steak. "Spot has to eat something." she explained unapologetically to all around. Jackpot!

The other day I was called in to see a child because of a "seizure." After observing the involuntary facial movements for a few moments I started going over in my mind the possible causes. Tetanus, botulisim, unusual seizure disorder etc. then I asked the mother if the child was taking any kind of medicine. Yes, he was taking Ritalin and Haldol for Attention Deficit Disorder (ADD). The child looked normal and healthy after the appropriate treatment for the drug induced reaction, but the mother insisted that he had all the symptoms of ADD. A couple of hours later the nurse told me that the same mother was in with another child having the same problem. I went in to look at the older child and saw the same involuntary facial movements. The child owned up to having taken a pink pill a few hours earlier. The mother then pulled out of her purse a bottle of pink Haldol pills. This child also had ADD as well as another younger sibling. ADD has become epidemic in the country since the Department of Human services has started rewarding families with ADD by giving them monthly cash prizes. That family had bingoed three times.

I was sent to the store once as a child to get a sack of pinto beans. When I returned home and proudly showed my mother the extra ten cents the grocer had given me by mistake her reply was, "Get back down to that store and give that ten cents back to him!" Back down the street I marched in that hot July sun the half-mile to the store. So much for the idea of Jackpots in the pre-welfare days!

Gambling has become as commonly accepted today as the welfare check. When I was a child growing up, both were considered as curses to society. Even the rich are playing the welfare bingo games today. I heard recently about a well off farmer who conned his poorer farmer neighbor into signing up on his crop program but when the government jackpot check came he refused to share it with the poorer farmer. That otherwise hard working and basically honest farmer had been reduced to a liar, cheat and common thief because of the temptations of the government sponsored jackpot mentality.

Gambling and the government give-away programs have risen simultaneously to produce a national Jackpot Mentality which is robbing our society of its moral and ethical foundations. The rushing torrent of money flowing out of Washington is undermining not only our morals but the respect for honest work which is one of the bedrocks of our American civilization. A couple of years ago I needed some strawberry pickers so asked a welfare mother who was in the emergency department if she knew of anyone interested. She replied, "My family ain't going to do that kind of work. That's low down work!"

Some of the ramifications of the health welfare system are rather interesting. The other day a woman came into the Emergency room with a broken arm. It had been broken in Washington State but as her Tenncaid was not accepted out there she drove all the way back to her home in Tennessee to get it X-rayed and treated. Of course she paid cash for the gas, colas, cigarettes, food and other commodities all the way across the country but she had been brainwashed into believing that she should not pay a penny for a vital matter such as her health. It is not uncommon for a person (on welfare) to come into the emergency room where it cost between $100 to $200 for a minimal visit when all they want is a prescription for aspirin or a simple cold remedy.

A while back my brother-in-law gave me a guided tour of the Center for Disease Control (CDC) in Atlanta where he worked. Naturally I was impressed with that fine institution. The good they do at the CDC, however, is not a drop in the bucket compared to the Program for Disease Promotion (PDP) headquartered in Washington D.C. The PDP which includes all the social and health welfare programs Washington runs, produces far more disease, physical and social, than any that is cured by their misguided efforts. A good example is the disease ridden welfare-dependent Pima Indians in Arizona who should be compared with their healthy welfare-free cousins across the border in Mexico.

Suppose I conducted a test of a new drug and during the test it was found that the drug was causing more deaths and problems that it was curing. If I didn't stop the experiment immediately people would be on my back quicker than a chicken on a June bug, but any kind of government program can go on doing its damage with hardly a complaint.

My friend Bob and I were working on a barn the other day. As is usually the custom when break time came we got into a heated political conversation. I had just finished a tirade on the evils of the welfare state and Bob for the most part agreed with me but dissented with, "But I don't like to see anyone hungry." "Bob," I asked, "When did you last see anyone hungry or even on the verge of being hungry?" He hemmed and hawed. Then I asked him if he had ever been hungry as a child. Yes, he remembered being hungry as a child when times were hard. I looked him over and said that it was obvious that the bit of hunger he experienced hadn't hurt him or else he couldn't have attained a 6' 2" stature. After a bit more discussion he finally came up with a local citizen long since passed of whom it was said that he starved to death. He went on to admit that he died with a pocket full of money and was too stingy to spend money on food.

On our break that day I explained to Bob that actually hunger is healthy, especially in our society today. Hunger promotes good health. Hunger promotes good work habits. Hunger promotes economic betterment. Hunger is conducive to a better moral climate. In fact I told Bob that our national motto should be "Hunger is Healthy". We should go about seeking a way to brainwash people into equating hunger with pleasure for such would be a giant leap forward in the fight against disease. Of course I am talking only about America now and not about Bangladesh or Rwanda.

Perhaps you think I am mean spirited with talk of hunger but having been born to a jobless father in the middle of the depression there are some memories. Hungry hobos would frequently come to our poor home (poor in money but rich in generosity) looking for a bite to eat. If they were hungry enough to work, then Mother would prepare them a hot meal of whatever was available. If they didn't have time to work, then they would be given anything handy but something at least. I well remember our frequent meals of cooked dried lima beans, cornbread and turnip greens. We might have been hungry at times but none of us six kids were obese and we all learned to work even if it was "low down work." And in those days we slept soundly at night with the doors open. Screen doors were only latched when the wind was blowing.

It is time to get rid of the Jackpot Welfare Mentality and bring back the lean hungry look so we could see poverty and disease on the run rather than gaining on us.

Before leaving welfare something should be mentioned of the mind-boggling waste of welfare. My old "Riverboat Gambler" patient from medical school told me of how he felt after a wild wasteful weekend of his younger days. He would hit town on a Friday night with his pockets full of money and come Monday morning all that would be left was, "two empty pockets, a black bottom and the wild willie jeebies." Increasingly more people are waking up these days with two empty pockets as the tax rate inches toward 50%. If we all could look inside the health system and see the cost of free riders either on a trivial pursuit or seeking relief from their self-induced illnesses, we would all have a quivering case of the "wild willie jeebies" as we learned where that 50% of our hard earned money went.

A DAILY DOSE OF DISCIPLINE
-CHAPTER 11-

The Fat Farmer kept up a continual barrage of questions as I squatted in front of him examining his hurting knee. The problem had already been seen by another doctor who x-rayed it and explained the pathology to him, but apparently he wasn't satisfied. I was well aware of the bulging belly protruding in my direction as I palpated the knee and listened to his queries. Not finding anything but some generalized tenderness I stopped my exam and looked up above that enormous waistline and asked, "If you plant corn what do you expect to harvest?" "Corn, of course." he replied. "That's what is called reaping what you sow." I said, to which he agreed. "Suppose you add sideboards to your truck and load it with corn several times its weight capacity. What happens then?" He told me that it would break a spring or an axle. I went on with, "Again that is what is called reaping what you sow." Unenthusiastically he nodded in agreement for I think he was beginning to get the point. I went on to explain that overloading the knees will cause the cartilage to crush leading to chronic arthritis with all its painful results. The Fat Farmer then admitted that the other doctor had told him the same thing but, never mind, he had medicaid so another consult didn't cost him anything.

Within a few minutes of setting out to convince the patient that his road to painless walking lay in taking off those sideboards and reducing his load, his wife walked into the room. A glance at her informed me that her culinary pursuits equalled those of her husband. I then sank into a slough of despair, realizing that I was in all likelihood engaged in a futile endeavor. In a meeker mood I continued my little lecture but despaired of inspiring dietary discipline in those two. In my depression a vision of the future crossed my mind. There was a knee replacement at horrendous cost. then disability for the remainder of his life. Later would come complications of diabetes including hypertension and maybe eye complications. If he survived the heart attack there would be a cardiac bypass. That belly would be a multimillion dollar mass before it was over. All of that for a lack of discipline.

After about forty years of medicine I have come to the conclusion that the diseases of non-discipline (self-induced) comprise about 80% of the disease in this country. Here I am referring to the total dollar amount of diseases and not just the number of office visits that would include sore throats and such that are cheap items in the total health budget. Some doctors may disagree with me and I will not quibble about the exact percentage, but remember that I am looking at things from the viewpoint of having practiced extensively in countries where almost all of the expensive diseases that we have in this country are practically nonexistent. Being absent in those populations leads me to believe that they are unnecessarily present in our population.

The reason for the absence of our citified diseases in the population that I worked with in Thailand is that their culture is conducive to good health. Their agriculture is labor intensive, their diet is simple and naturally non-fattening and their social mores preclude sexual promiscuity. Their road to good health doesn't require discipline but comes naturally because of their circumstances. In America we have a vastly different set of circumstances which are conducive to the citified diseases which happen to be a very expensive set of diseases owing to their chronic nature. The expense of these diseases is intensified by our rapidly advancing medical technology that keeps the patient alive just a little longer.

The naturally occurring diseases such as childhood diseases, intestinal parasites and malaria which ravage primitive cultures have been almost completely eliminated from our culture. Immunizations, good hygiene and sanitation have culled the diseases in our country leaving mainly the self-induced diseases which will require self-discipline as the major tool to fight the diseases of the new age.

Discipline is a difficult concept in this period of new age permissiveness. A while back I was trying to impress on a smoking obese hypertensive patient the need to change her habits for the sake of controlling her hypertension. I hadn't made much progress when she defended herself by saying, "I only have two bad habits. Don't you have any bad habits?" It is amazing how many people feel entitled to have a bad habit or two. It is not unusual for those, as they began to reap what they sow, to feel entitled to have someone else pay for the consequences of their habits. God created us and destined us to be disciplined not entitled to a bad habit or a free lunch.

Just as discipline is a dirty word today there is a loathing of anything that smacks of struggle and suffering as if they were some kind of a curse. Suffering, struggle and discipline create the substance and strength of our society. Just as it is essential for the butterfly to struggle to escape the cacoon it is necessary for man to endure disciplined effort for the sake of good health.

We are all surrounded by circumstances which, in spite of constitutional guarantees, are not equal. Regardless of our diverse environments and various gene pools, we are all born with the power to struggle one step at a time upward if that be the direction we have chosen. Take for instance the heredity and circumstances into which a baby appeared a hundred and fifty years ago. Born of a slave mother, George Washington Carver kept going upward all his life until he became one of the greatest Americans in our history. He looked through the suffering of his circumstances to see the face of God. With that daily encounter he could stare into any situation with discipline and determination. Compassion and concern grew in that hothouse of suffering and when it came time for a decision, he opted to teach in a poor rural Southern school where with his master's degree in agriculture he blessed thousands with his humble servant-like spirit. Sure, Carver had some help along the way but basically discipline made him successful.

Welfare doesn't teach discipline but dependency. Hand in hand with dependency is wastefulness that develops in the welfare mind as one labors, not for gain, but for things freely given. It should be no surprise that the undisciplined drift to the lower end of the economic spectrum where the welfare state will then keep them enslaved in dependency and wastefulness.

Often in trying to convince patients to stop unhealthy habits I invoke their children by telling them that discipline is one of the greatest gifts that they can pass on to their offspring. Misery is the almost constant companion of the undisciplined whether it be in their marriage and family life, workplace or in their health. Discipline in health is more important now than ever before and those who refuse discipline are almost guaranteed to suffer poor health.

Dr. Dean Ornish demonstrated the benefits of discipline even on poor health a few years ago. He took a group of patients with severely advanced cardiac disease. They were put on a very strict regimen of diet, exercise, and stress reduction. Atheromatous lesions in the arteries at the end of the study period had reduced in size. Some who had been cardiac cripples were hiking in the mountains. The dramatic improvement was the result of a disciplined approach to health one which anyone can take if he so chooses.

We are living now in an age where disease depends increasingly on discipline or the lack thereof. The government cannot legislate discipline nor can the corporations or insurance companies. Discipline is a matter of the individual will. If that be the case is it just or wise to spread the cost of one's disease onto others who are disciplined? Is present government welfare reasonable? Is health insurance of a private nature even reasonable unless there are incentives built into it to punish unhealthy behavior and encourage healthy habits? If we want health reform we had better look first at where the problems are and then launch a disciplined attack.

MEDICAL QUACKERY
-CHAPTER 12-

The last lecture of medical school was a presentation by the ex-Dean on the subject of medical quackery. This lecture was a highly entertaining session as well as a warning of things that we would encounter in our practices. And over the span of my medical career in medicine there has been and continues to be abundant examples of medical quackery. The ultimate form of medical quackery, though is that brought about by the politicians in the form of government medicine. Oh, it sounds good that everyone is entitled to equal medical care under one great umbrella just as the sound of all medical quacks as they offer a panacea for that which ails a suffering soul.

One of the few things that I remember from my college philosophy class of over 60 years ago are the words of the professor who said, "Communism will fail because it ignores human nature." Communism is only one form of socialism which fails everywhere it is experimented with, and more than the failure it brings misery to the masses who expected a cure for all their ailments. The siren allurement to ignore our own human nature is repeated over and over in history, for to believe in things as we feel they "ought to be" rather than the way they really are is the gold mine of the medical quack.

Inherent in a government run health care system is the widespread and ever present temptation to act irresponsibly, which as we see today makes the cost of the system impossibly expensive. In my 25 years of emergency medical practice there was a continual stream of patients demanding medical care for trivial matters because they had "insurance." Of course they had insurance, which was medicaid or medicare for which they had not paid a dime toward the policy. But it was their "right" so the care was given and since it was care in the emergency department it was at great expense to the taxpayer.

A good example of the irresponsible use of "free medicine" was seen at a military facility where I worked briefly. The waiting room of the emergency department was as large as a small auditorium and filled day and night. A military family may be out for a drive when suddenly as they passed the hospital one of the parents would realize that they were out of aspirin so the family whipped into the E R waiting room to wait for the doctor to see them and give them a script for aspirin which was free to the military. Anyone with any mental capacity at all should be able to see that when a person pays the doctor out of his own pocket he will act in a much more responsible manner.

Another way the patient acts irresponsibly is simply by his choice to live irresponsibly. Being overweight and not exercising are personal choices that lead to medical problems that can be extremely costly. There are many areas of life activities where a person would be very careful to act in a responsible manner if he were to be responsible for all of the consequences of those actions. If the patient bears no burden of the consequences of his behavior then, "Why worry?" Just let someone else pay the bill. To ignore human nature is pure folly, but folly is changed to compassion in the politician's mind.

Physicians and others providing health services are another source of massive cost overruns in a government run health care system. Most physicians that I have known are careful to order only tests, procedures, and medicines that are necessary in the care of their patients. The deep pockets of any insurance program makes for a powerful temptation to over prescribe in various ways. Procedures, used for example in the field of gastroenterology and cardiology, are very lucrative and easily justified in follow-up visits. When some other party is paying the bill for the patient, then there is strong temptation to order more to run up a larger bill. In the days when the physician was paid directly by the patient the physician was much more careful to order only what was necessary. Moreover in the case of a patient with limited means the physician was even more careful in the use of medical tests and procedures.

In the past few years billing by doctors and medial facilities has become extremely complex. Each disease and procedure has a code as determined by the insurance companies and the correct code must be used to insure reimbursement. A physician's office may contract with coding specialists who make regular visits to the office to examine the charts and make recommendations to the physicians that will improve coding and thus increase reimbursements from the insurance companies. In the emergency department where I worked we were continually reminded to make all the diagnoses possible for a patient and each diagnosis had to be backed up by detailed history and physical. Simplicity is no longer the order as complexity metastasizes throughout the system. All of this complexity is for the purpose of increasing the amount of the bill for the patient's visit. Billing codes become more and more the focus in the equation and the patient and his disease becomes less important.

A friend asked about one of his doctors that had gone to work in another city. Another person knowledgeable about the situation allowed that that doctor had been charged with billing for patients that he had not seen. Fraud on a massive scale is one of the usual and customary accoutrements of a government health care system. The temptation is too great and human nature being what it is cannot withstand the enticement. Billing between the doctor and his patient may at times not be completely honest but it will never reach the scale that it is in a government run system.

The insertion of insurance between the patient and the physician results in irresponsible behavior on the part of both parties leading to massive increased costs of medical care. A simple system based on a personal relationship between doctor and patient (hospital and patient) keeps the cost at a minimal level.

The insertion of insurance be it public (government) or private adds expenses that are ever increasing. Rules and regulations must be written and rewritten continually to keep reimbursement organized properly. Those writing the rules and regulations eventually get into the area of regulating the tests, procedures, and medicines ordered by the physician and that "insertion" which started with simple insurance becomes more ominous as the personal relationship between the doctor and patient becomes more tenuous. The ever-changing regulations require compliance officers in each institution to be continually reviewing the regulations so the institution can avoid fines and even going to jail for failing to "comply." The doctor who should be completely devoted to the solving of the patient's ailments now has to be concerned with keeping out of jail.

The temptation to fraudulently bill the insurance systems leads to the addition of a policing system to discover the evil-doers. Here is another layer of expense in the medical care system that would not be necessary if there are only the doctor and patient involved in the payment process. Only a few of the "layers" (and there are many) have been mentioned, all of which add to the financial burden of the system and take money away from the actual patient healing process.

The Health and Human Services Department is a non-elected branch of government, which has jurisdiction over Medicare and Medicaid. They write all the rules and regulations which if not followed may result in severe fines or jail sentences. All the while it is a "shadow government" unresponsive to the taxpayer. A non-elected department writing laws governing such a large part of our economy is of course foreign to our representative form of government.

Free health care for all sounds so good and it is good

for some and for a time but the end of the experiment in folly seems in sight. "There is a way that seems right to a man but in the end it leads to death" (Proverbs 14:12) My philosophy professor's quote "Communism will fail because it ignores human nature." should be applied to our brand of socialism as it too ignores human nature.

The last statement in the lecture of the ex-Dean is remembered quite well, "Gentlemen remember this. Knowledge is the foam that washes up on the beach and ignorance is the ocean that remains after it has melted away." I have no notion that the politicians in Washington will cease from their endeavors to tweak the health system as we have it today. The tweaking will eventually result in a giant TWANG as our economy comes to a grinding halt. The ignorance of ignoring human nature will eventually overwhelm the little bit of knowledge that we have accumulated.

"It is amazing that people who think we cannot afford to pay for doctors, hospitals, and medication somehow think that we can afford to pay for doctors, hospitals, medication, and a government bureaucracy to admisister it."

-Thomas Sowell

"The point at which good intentions exceed the power to fullfill them marked for the culture the onset of decadence."

-Jacques Barzun* (1907-2012)

*From his book "From Dawn to Decadence 500 Years of Western Cultural Life."
This quote is on page 779 in the final chaper entitled Demotic Life and Times. It is
highly recommended reading as Barzun describes our times.